Toucans

By Sam Dollar

Raintree

ANIMALS OF THE RAINFOREST

www.raintreepublishers.co.uk
Visit our website to find out more information about Raintree books.

To order:
☎ Phone 44 (0) 1865 888112
🖹 Send a fax to 44 (0) 1865 314091
💻 Visit the Raintree Bookshop at www.raintreepublishers.co.uk to browse our catalogue and order online.

First published in Great Britain by Raintree Publishers, Halley Court, Jordan Hill, Oxford, OX2 8EJ, part of Harcourt Education.
Raintree is a registered trademark of Harcourt Education Ltd.

Originated by Dot Gradations Ltd
Printed and bound in Hong Kong and China by South China

ISBN 1 844 21092 8
07 06 05 04 03
10 9 8 7 6 5 4 3 2 1

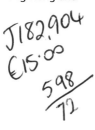

British Library Cataloguing in Publication Data
Dollar, Sam
Toucans - (Animals of the rainforest)
1. Toucans - Juvenile literature
2. Rainforest ecology - Juvenile literature
I.Title
598.7'2
A catalogue for this book is available from the British Library.

Acknowledgements
The publishers would like to thank the following for permission to reproduce photographs:
Martin Vince, pp. **16, 20, 22, 24** (top and bottom); Photo Network/Mark Newman, p. **15**; NHPA, pp . **7, 10**; Photophile, pp. **4–5**; Anthony Mercieca, p. **18**; Unicorn Stock Photos/Tommy Dodson, p. **29**; Tom Ulrich, pp. **1, 12**; Fritz Pölking, p. **8**; William Grenfell, p. **11**; Inga Spence, p. **25**; Wildlife Conservation Society/Diane Shapiro, p. **26**.

Cover photograph by Visuals Unlimited/ James Beveridge.

Every effort has been made to contact copyright holders of any material reproduced in this book. Any omissions will be rectified in subsequent printings if notice is given to the publishers.

Contents

Any words appearing in the text in bold, **like this**, are explained in the Glossary.

plumage
see pages 14, 19

small wings
see page 13

large bill
see pages 9, 13, 18

legs and feet
see page 13

USA

MEXICO

BELIZE
GUATEMALA
HONDURAS
EL SALVADOR
NICARAGUA
COSTA RICA
PANAMA

Caribbean Sea

North Atlantic
Ocean

VENEZUELA
GUYANA
SURINAM
FRENCH GUIANA

COLOMBIA

ECUADOR

Amazon River

PERU

BRAZIL

BOLIVIA

PARAGUAY

South Pacific
Ocean

URUGUAY

ARGENTINA

CHILE

South Atlantic
Ocean

N
W   E
S

Range of the toucan
Surrounding land
Sea
Borders
Rivers

A quick look at toucans

What do toucans look like?

Toucans are colourful birds with large **bills**. An average toucan bill is about 20 centimetres long.

Where do toucans live?

Toucans live in South America and Central America. They live in the treetops of rainforests.

What do toucans eat?

Toucans eat mainly fruit. They sometimes eat insects and small animals.

Do toucans have any enemies?

Eagles, hawks, ocelots and snakes eat toucans. Many animals eat toucans' eggs.

This toucan is resting on a branch high in the treetops.

Toucans in the rainforest

Toucans are birds that live in South and Central America. They have colourful feathers and large banana-shaped beaks called bills. A toucan's bill can be as long as its body.

Toucans are colourful birds. There are more than 35 kinds of toucans. Each kind has different colours. Their feathers can be white, red, blue, green, black, yellow, orange and brown.

Many toucans live in **Amazonia**. This is the world's largest rainforest. It grows around the the river Amazon in South America. It is home to more than 1600 kinds of birds.

Toucans are an important part of the rainforest. They spit out the seeds from the fruits they eat. New trees grow from the seeds. This helps the rainforest spread to new places.

Toucans travel around the rainforest with other toucans. A group of toucans is called a flock. There are usually between four and twelve toucans in a flock. They sleep, eat and even play together.

Where toucans live

Toucans live in most areas of South and Central America. Most kinds of toucans live in lowland rainforest **habitats**. A habitat is a place where an animal or plant usually lives and grows. It is very warm in the lowlands. But a few kinds of toucan live in mountain forests. It is cooler in the mountains.

Toucans live in the forest **canopy** about 46 metres above the ground. The canopy is a thick area of leaves high up in the treetops. It is like a giant umbrella of leaves and branches.

Toucans rarely leave the forest canopy because everything they need is there. Different kinds of fruits grow on the trees. Water collects on leaves and tree branches. Toucans fly or hop to different tree branches to find food and water.

Toucans are heavy birds. They sit on thick branches because thin branches might break.

Toucans sometimes fly to different parts of the rainforest.

Special body parts

Toucans have large, brightly coloured bills. A toucan's bill might have several patches of different colours on it. This makes the toucan easy to recognize.

An average toucan bill is about 20 centimetres long. But it is hollow and very light. The birds use their bills to pick fruits from high branches.

Toucans' feet and legs help them move around the rainforest. Their feet have two claws at the front and two at the back. These claws allow toucans to grip branches. Toucans also have powerful legs. Their strong legs help them hop from branch to branch.

Toucans' wings are short and round. These help them keep their balance as they move from tree to tree. Toucans also use their wings to fly to different parts of the rainforest.

Groups of toucans

Scientists have divided toucans into four main groups. These groups are the Ramphastos, Aracaris, Toucanets and mountain toucans. Each kind of toucan fits into one of these groups.

Toucans in the Ramphastos group are the largest toucans. They have mainly black **plumage**. Plumage is a bird's feathers. Toco toucans belong to the Ramphastos group.

Toucans in the Aracaris group are small and thin. They have smaller bills than the larger Ramphastos toucans. Red-necked aracaris belong to the Aracaris group. They have a bright yellow band across their chests.

Toucans in the Toucanet group often have bright green plumage. They live in both cool mountain forests and lowland rainforests. Emerald toucanets belong to the Toucanet group. Their bright green plumage gives them **camouflage**. Camouflage is colouring that helps an animal blend in with the things around it, such as the green leaves in the canopy.

This large toucan is a member of the Ramphastos group.

Toucans in the mountain toucan group live in the Andes mountains and other South American mountains.

Black-billed mountain toucans belong to the mountain toucan group. They have special colouring. They have brown backs and wings and pale blue bellies. No other toucan group has this pale blue colouring.

This adult toucan is feeding insects to its young.

Survival

Toucans are **omnivores**. They eat both animals and plants. Toucans' bills are lighter and not as hard as some other birds. They are not able to crunch hard food well. Like all birds, toucans have no teeth to chew food.

Toucans eat mainly soft fruits. Many different fruits grow all year in the warm rainforest. In the wild, toucans eat about a hundred different kinds of fruits, including berries and bananas.

Toucans feed insects and animals to their young to help them grow. These include termites, spiders and even lizards, snakes and baby birds.

This toucan has found a tree with plenty of fruit to eat.

Finding food and eating

Toucans use their long bills to pick fruits that are hard to reach. Their bills also have small ridges. These ridges are like the blade of a saw. Toucans use the ridges to cut chunks out of pieces of fruit.

Toucans sometimes eat young birds. They wave their bills around to scare away adult birds from their nests. Then toucans eat the young birds left in the nests.

Toucans swallow their food whole. Getting food to their throats can be hard because their bills are so long. A toucan takes a piece of fruit in its bill. Then it raises its head up in the air. This makes the fruit slide from the tip of its bill down to its throat.

Escaping from predators

Toucans' plumage helps them hide from **predators**. Predators hunt and eat other animals. Larger birds, such as eagles and hawks, eat toucans. Toucans' colourful feathers help them blend in with their surroundings. They can sit still on tree branches and look like flowers.

Predators have a hard time seeing toucans at night. Toucans sleep with their heads turned around backwards. They lay their bills over their backs. Then they tip their tails up to cover their bills. They sleep this way so that many toucans can fit on one tree branch. This way of sleeping hides toucans from predators because their bills are hidden in their feathers. Predators do not realize that the sleeping toucans are birds.

A toucan's life cycle

Toucans mate during the warm, rainy season. Males put on a show to attract female toucans. They sing and fluff up their feathers to show off their colours. They wave their bills up and down.

Bill fencing is often a part of mating. This toucan mating practice was named after the sport of fencing. In fencing, people fight with long, thin swords. In bill fencing, a male toucan uses his bill to hit a female's bill. The female uses her bill to hit him back.

◀ **Toucans wave their bills up and down to attract other toucans.**

This toucan is on a branch outside its nest. The nest opening is in the tree.

Nesting

Toucans search for places to build their nests after they have attracted mates. Making a nest together is an important part of mating.

All toucans build nests high above the ground inside holes in trees. Toucans' bills are not hard enough to make nesting holes in trees. They must find existing holes. Small toucans use old woodpecker or parrot holes. Large toucans are too big to fit in these holes. Instead, they must use rotten patches in trees.

Males and females work together to make a nest chamber inside the opening. The chamber must be large enough to hold several eggs. Toucans use their bills to dig out rotten wood or plants. This makes the opening larger.

Females are ready to lay eggs about two weeks after mating. They lay between two and four white eggs.

Protecting the nest

Predators try to find toucan nests. Eagles, weasels, monkeys and other animals eat eggs and young toucans. Adult toucans try to hide their nests from predators. They will not fly to their nests if they see predators nearby.

Toucans do not fight to protect the nest if predators find them. They fly away. Toucans would be killed if they tried to fight predators.

Nestlings

Toucan eggs hatch in about eighteen days.
Newly hatched toucans are called **nestlings**.
Nestlings have short bills and bare pink skin.
Thick pads of skin around their ankles protect
them from the rough floor of the nest chamber.

Nestlings grow slowly. Their eyes stay
closed for three weeks. The parents take
care of the nestlings while they grow.
They feed them at least five times a day.
They keep the nest clean by scooping
waste into their bills. They then fly out
of the nest and dump the waste. One of
the parents sleeps with the nestlings at
night. This keeps the nestlings warm.

It takes about seven weeks for
nestlings to grow their feathers. The
young birds are then called **fledglings**.
They are able to fly. The pads on their
ankles begin to disappear. Fledglings
have short, pale coloured bills.

Top: these newly hatched toucans still have
their eyes closed. *Bottom*: this 13-day-old
toucan has no feathers yet.

This fledgling has grown some feathers and is able to fly.

Young toucans are in danger from predators. Fledglings are weak and cannot protect themselves. Adult toucans do not fight to protect them either.

Young toucans usually grow to become healthy adults if they escape predators. Most toucans live for about sixteen years.

Toucans spend a great deal of time cleaning their feathers. Some people use toucan feathers to make things.

Living with toucans

People and toucans have been living together for thousands of years. In Amazonia, toucans have been an important food for people. Some people also make things out of toucans' feathers. Some of the people of Amazonia believe that toucans have special powers.

Today, toucans are popular birds in many parts of the world. People visit zoos and bird **sanctuaries** to see toucans. Some artists paint or draw pictures of toucans. People buy toucan calendars and toucan postcards. One cereal company uses a cartoon toucan on its boxes and in its advertisements.

Pet toucans

Some toucans never live in the wild. People raise toucans to sell as pets. Toucans are popular pets. They cannot talk like parrots, but they are clever birds. People can teach them tricks such as rolling over and playing fetch or catch.

Toucans need lots of room to exercise. They must have large cages so that they can fly around in them, or they must be given the chance to fly every day.

Toucans in danger

Hunting puts toucans in danger. People hunt toucans for food. Others hunt them for their colourful feathers and bills. Some people use toucans' bills to make medicines.

The main danger to toucans is rainforest destruction. People are cutting down many trees in the rainforest to build homes and farms. Toucans live in the trees of the rainforest. Without the rainforest, toucans cannot live in the wild.

Toucans need rainforest trees to live in the wild.

Glossary

Amazonia largest rainforest in the world

bill the beak of a bird

camouflage colours or markings that help an animal blend into its surroundings

canopy (KAN-uh-pee) thick area of leaves high up in the treetops

fledgling a young bird that has just grown its feathers and is able to fly

habitat place where an animal or plant naturally lives and grows

nestling newly hatched bird

omnivore animal that eats both animals and plants

plumage all of a bird's feathers

predator animal that hunts and eats other animals

sanctuary a nature, animal or plant reserve

More information

Internet sites

Rainforest Education
www.rainforestlive.org.uk

Really Wild Zone
www.bbc.co.uk/reallywild/amazing

Useful address

World Wildlife Fund-UK
Panda House, Weyside Park,
Godalming, Surrey, GU7 1XR

Books to read

Theodorou, R; Telford C. *Amazing Journeys:
Up a Rainforest Tree. Heinemann Library,
Oxford, 1998*

Index